W9-AZS-211

Fraction
ACTION

Lisa Arias

Rourke
Educational Media

rourkeeducationalmedia.com

*Scan for Related Titles
and Teacher Resources*

Before Reading:

Building Academic Vocabulary and Background Knowledge

Before reading a book, it is important to tap into what your child or students already know about the topic. This will help them develop their vocabulary, increase their reading comprehension, and make connections across the curriculum.

1. Look at the cover of the book. What will this book be about?
2. What do you already know about the topic?
3. Let's study the Table of Contents. What will you learn about in the book's chapters?
4. What would you like to learn about this topic? Do you think you might learn about it from this book? Why or why not?
5. Use a reading journal to write about your knowledge of this topic. Record what you already know about the topic and what you hope to learn about the topic.
6. Read the book.
7. In your reading journal, record what you learned about the topic and your response to the book.
8. After reading the book complete the activities below.

Content Area Vocabulary
Read the list. What do these words mean?

denominator

equivalent

fraction

fraction bar

half

improper fraction

mixed number

numerator

proper fraction

whole number

After Reading:

Comprehension and Extension Activity

After reading the book, work on the following questions with your child or students in order to check their level of reading comprehension and content mastery.

1. Explain the relationship between the numerator and denominator. (Summarize)
2. Why is the fraction smaller as the numerator and the denominator get farther apart? (Asking questions)
3. What are the rules when adding or subtracting fractions? (Summarize)
4. How do you use fractions in your life? (Text to self connection)
5. What are equivalent fractions? (Summarize)

Extension Activity

Let's explore fractions with candy! First you will need a bag of M&Ms or Skittles. Open the bag and pour onto a plate or clean table. Count the total number of candies, then group them according to color. Write the fraction for each color group on a piece of paper. Remember that the denominator is the total number of candies and the numerator is the number in the color group. After you write a fraction for each color group add them up! Do they add up to the total number of candies that were in the bag?

TABLE OF CONTENTS

What Is a Fraction? 4

Proper Fractions in Action 10

Mixed Numbers 16

Improper Fractions .18

Equivalent Fractions 20

Fraction Math 22

Glossary 30

Index 31

Websites to Visit 31

About the Author 32

WHAT IS A FRACTION?

Splitting a candy bar fairly would be hard to do
if fractions were not there for me and you.

Using fractions is smart.
Each part of a whole is split equally,
right from the start.

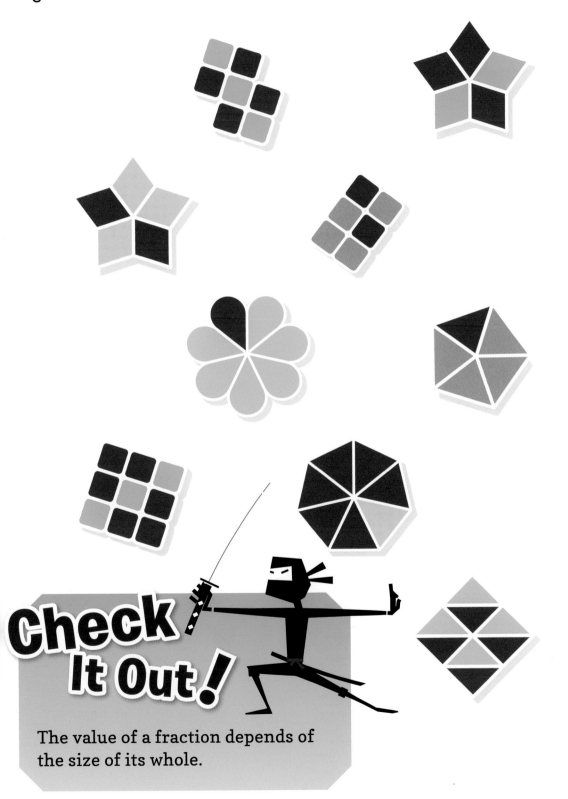

Check It Out!

The value of a fraction depends of
the size of its whole.

What Does a Fraction Look Like?

A **fraction bar** splits two numbers you see.
The **numerator** on top is as friendly as can be.
It has one important goal:
to show you how many parts are taken from the whole.

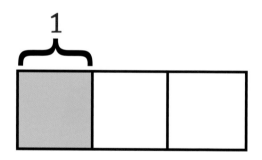

$$\frac{1}{3} \longleftarrow \text{Numerator}$$

The **denominator** is the number below the fraction bar.
It has one important goal:
to show how many parts are in the whole.

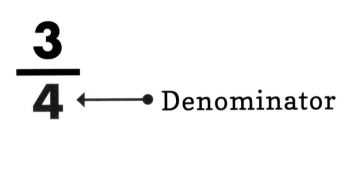

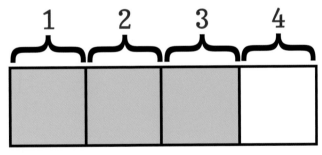

Practice Makes Perfect

Time to take some action to correctly say a **fraction**.
Always start with the numerator. Just say the number you see, carefully.

Next is the denominator. Take a moment to notice,
denominators are said with a bonus.

$$\frac{1}{5} = \text{one-fifth}$$

Denominator	What to Say
1	Whole
2	Half
3	Third
4	Fourth
5	Fifth
6	Sixth
7	Seventh
8	Eighth
9	Ninth
10	Tenth

Use the chart to correctly say these fraction parts.

PROPER FRACTIONS IN ACTION

We know that fractions are part of a whole. Let's take a minute to watch a **proper fraction** grow.

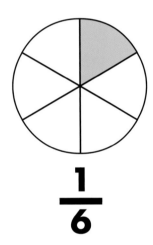

$$\frac{1}{6}$$

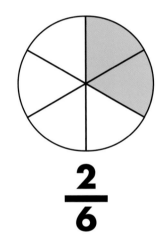

$$\frac{2}{6}$$

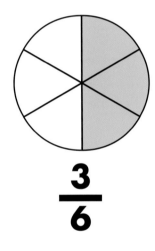

$$\frac{3}{6}$$

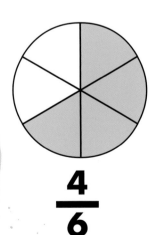

$$\frac{4}{6}$$

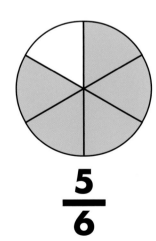

$$\frac{5}{6}$$

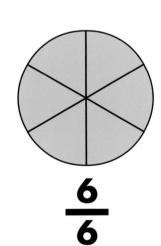

$$\frac{6}{6}$$

Now it is time to watch proper fractions on a number line.

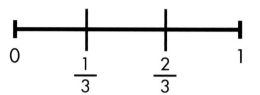

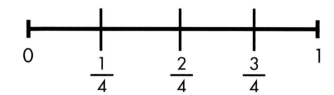

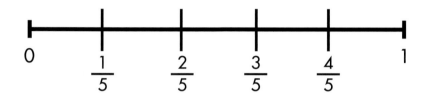

Can you guess the missing fraction on this number line?

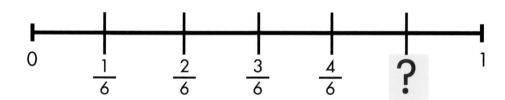

Check It Out!

When the numerator is smaller than the denominator, you have a proper fraction.

Answer: $\frac{5}{6}$

Compare and Order Fractions

Comparing and ordering a fraction starts
with observing a fraction's parts.
The closer the numerator and denominator become,
the fraction is nearer the **whole number** 1.

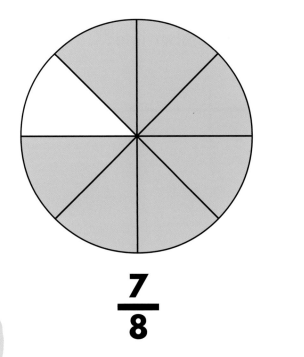

$$\frac{7}{8}$$

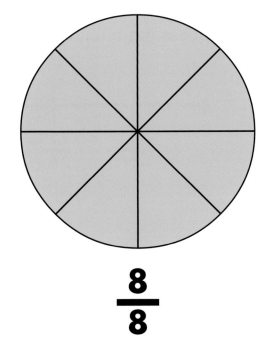

$$\frac{8}{8}$$

When the numerator and denominator are far apart,
the fraction is very small, almost nothing at all.

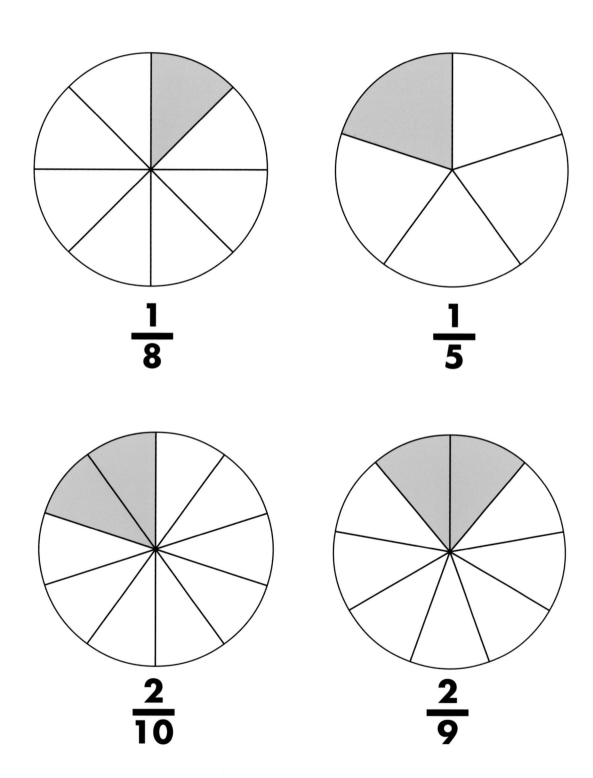

$$\frac{1}{8}$$

$$\frac{1}{5}$$

$$\frac{2}{10}$$

$$\frac{2}{9}$$

Uncovering one-**half** is very clear.
As long as the numerator is half the denominator, the fraction one-half will appear.

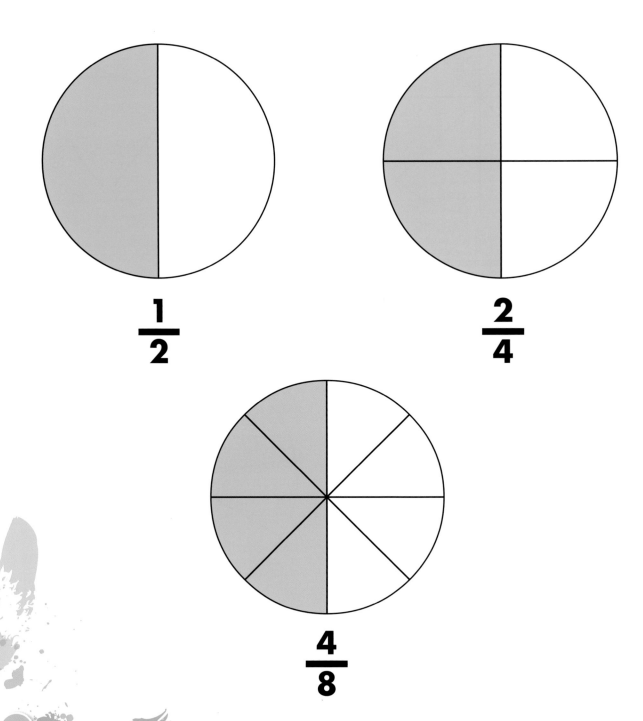

$$\frac{1}{2}$$

$$\frac{2}{4}$$

$$\frac{4}{8}$$

Decide if each fraction is closest to one, one-half, or none.

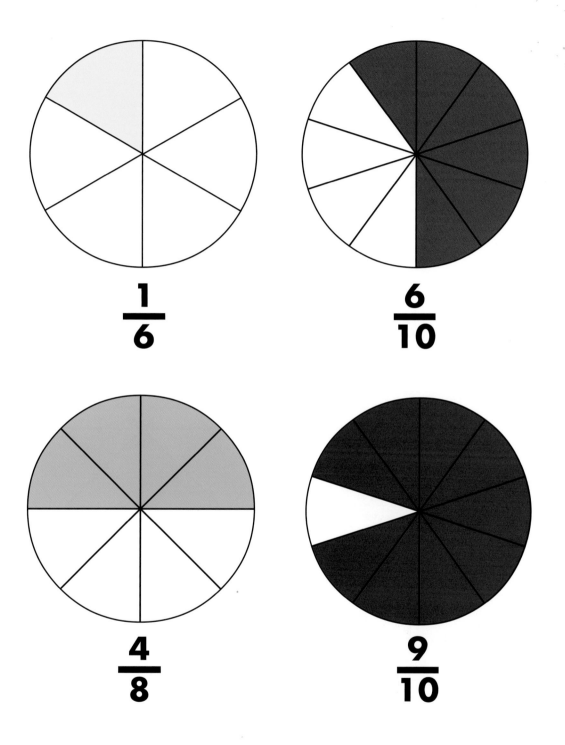

$$\frac{1}{6}$$

$$\frac{6}{10}$$

$$\frac{4}{8}$$

$$\frac{9}{10}$$

MIXED NUMBERS

Find out how it is a fun action
to join a **whole number** with a fraction.

The two wholes equal 2 and the third circle equals ⅛. Join them
together and your **mixed number** is, 2 ⅛.

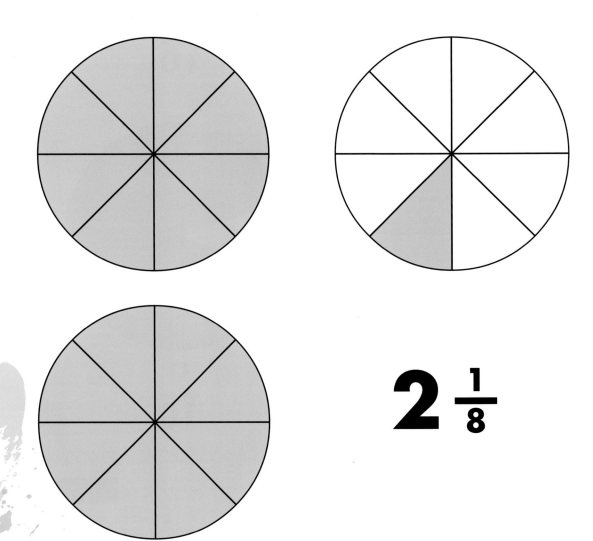

$$2 \frac{1}{8}$$

Now it is time for some mixed number fun.
Take a peek at each picture and guess its mixed number.

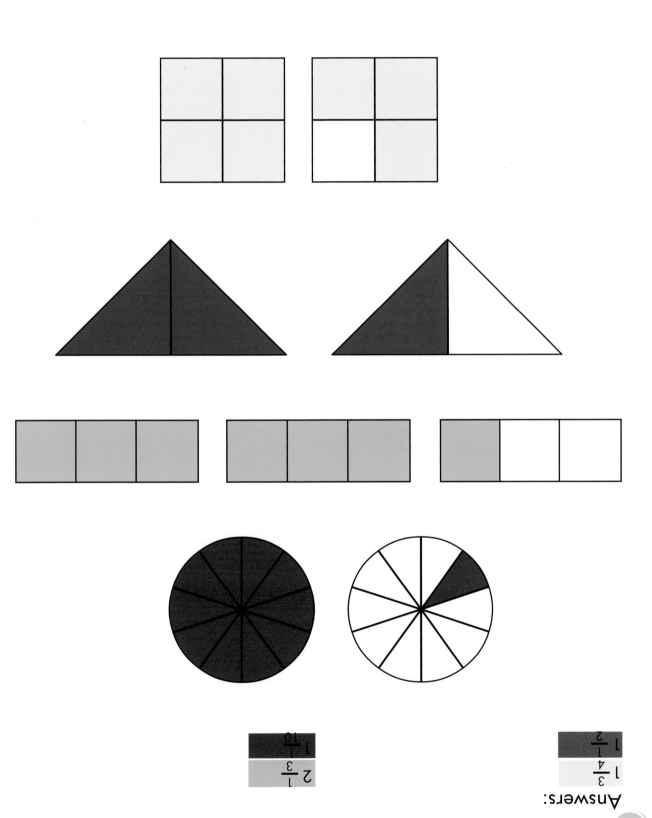

IMPROPER FRACTIONS

Time to cheer!

When the numerator is larger than the denominator an **improper fraction** is near.

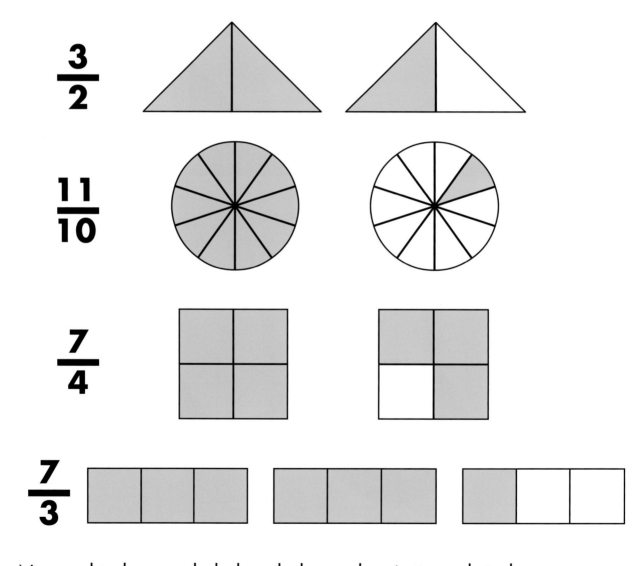

No need to be puzzled, the whole number just needs to be discovered.

Time to take some action.
Find each improper fraction.

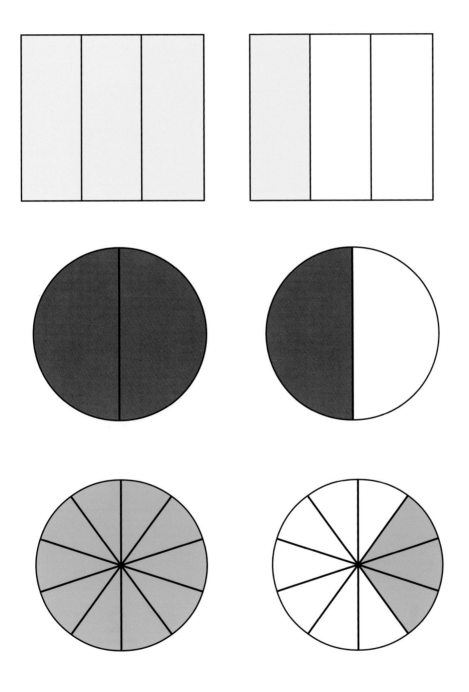

EQUIVALENT FRACTIONS

How can it be?
Fractions look so different but are thought of equally.

It will take just a moment to learn how fractions can be **equivalent**.

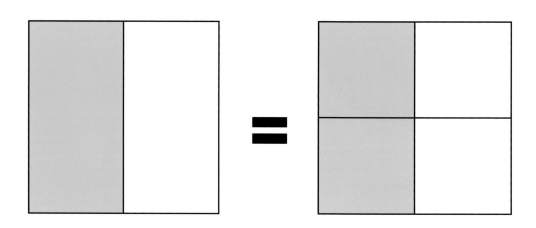

$$\frac{1}{2} \quad \text{is equal to} \quad \frac{2}{4}$$

It is so clever,
to show equivalent fractions together.

Look at the pictures or try the math to show
their equivalency.

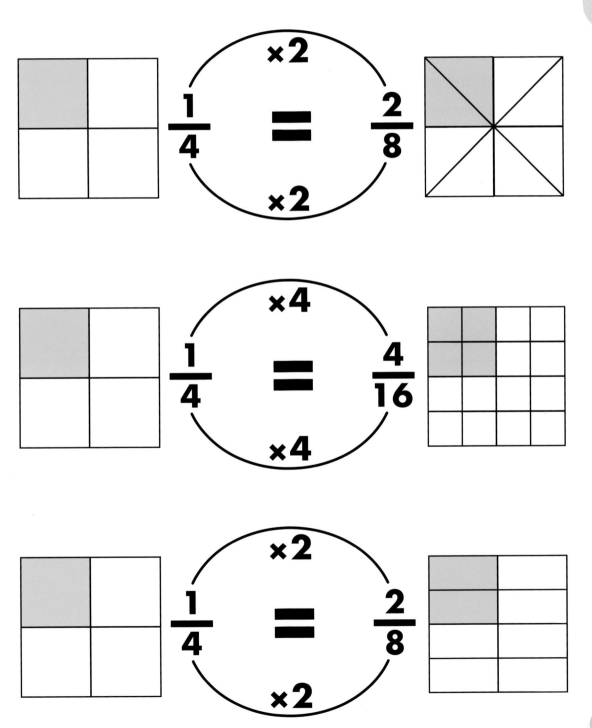

FRACTION MATH

Adding Fractions

I am so glad it is time to add.

Adding fractions with like denominators is quite tame.
Just add the numerators, keeping the denominators the same.

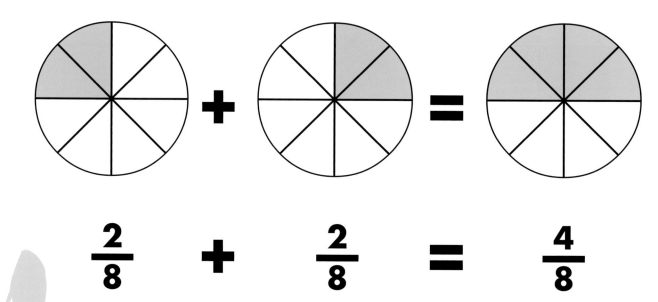

$$\frac{2}{8} \quad + \quad \frac{2}{8} \quad = \quad \frac{4}{8}$$

Add these fractions!

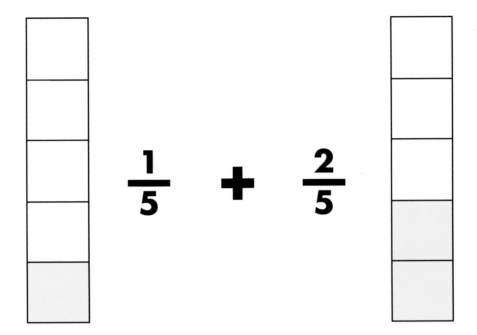

$$\frac{1}{5} + \frac{2}{5}$$

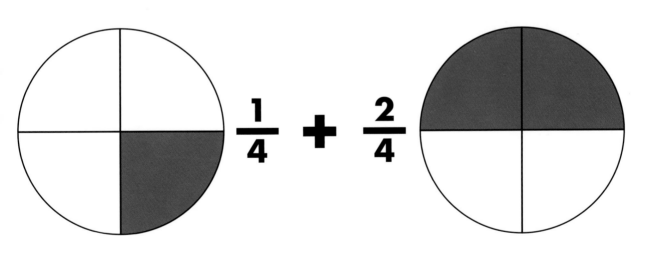

$$\frac{1}{4} + \frac{2}{4}$$

Subtracting Fractions

It is a fact. We are ready to subtract.

The rules are the same as adding. If the denominators are the same, subtract the numerators and the denominators will remain unchanged.

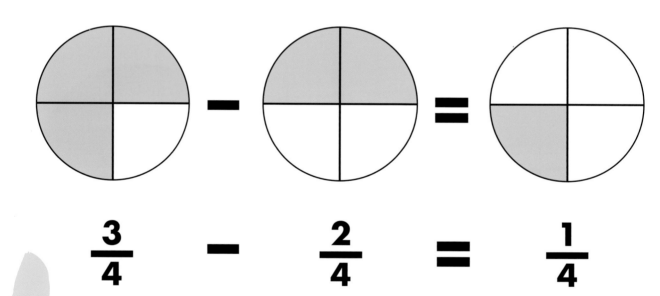

$$\frac{3}{4} - \frac{2}{4} = \frac{1}{4}$$

Subtract these fractions!

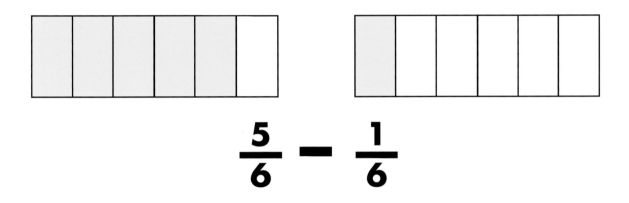

$$\frac{5}{6} - \frac{1}{6}$$

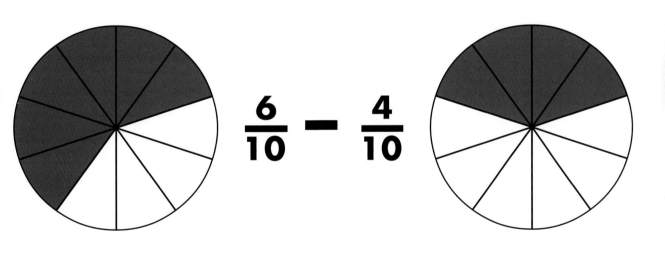

$$\frac{6}{10} - \frac{4}{10}$$

Compare Fractions

Time to compare fractions with the same denominator. The numerator controls how the fraction grows. Take a look and see how the numerator is key.

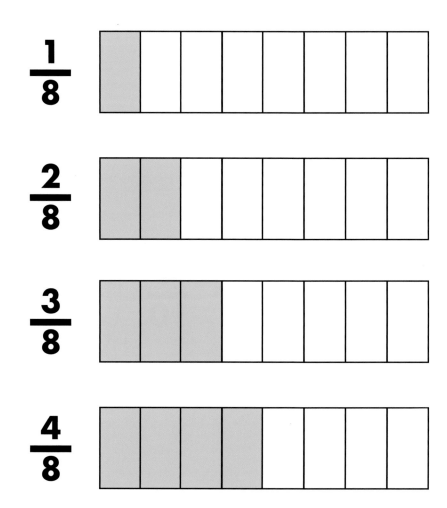

Order these fractions from least to greatest.

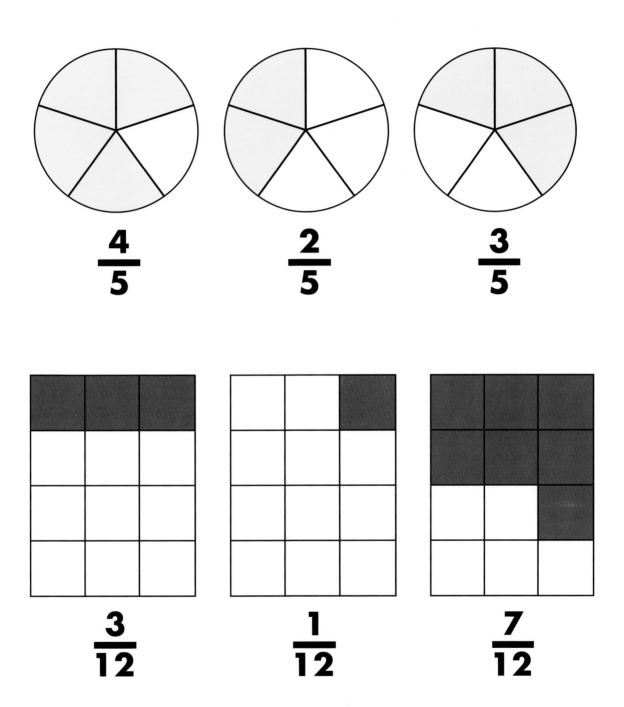

$$\frac{4}{5}$$

$$\frac{2}{5}$$

$$\frac{3}{5}$$

$$\frac{3}{12}$$

$$\frac{1}{12}$$

$$\frac{7}{12}$$

Time to compare fractions with the same numerator. The denominator's job is to split the whole. As the denominator becomes larger, each part left for the numerator gets smaller and smaller.

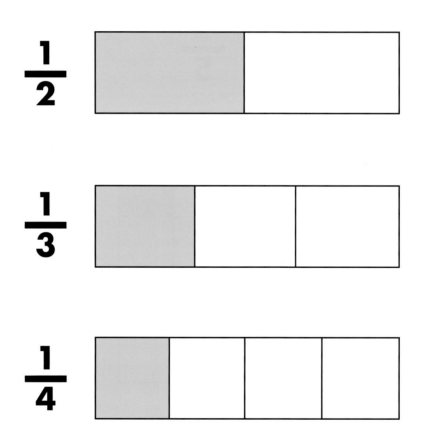

Order these fractions from least to greatest.

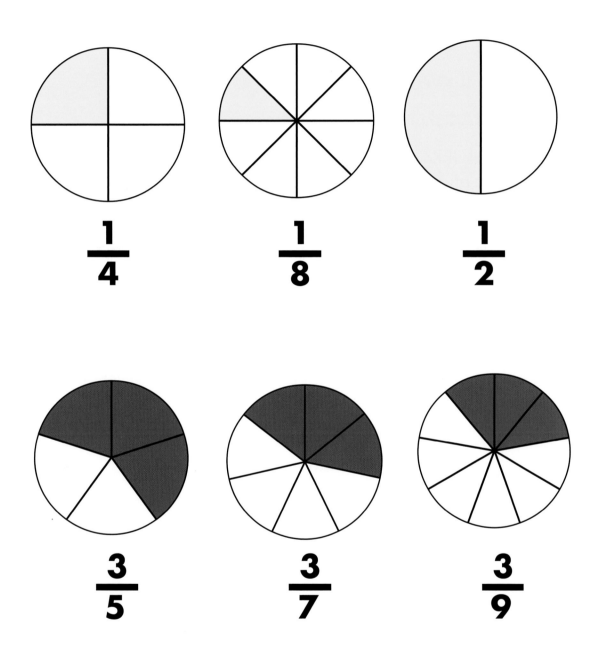

$$\frac{1}{4}$$

$$\frac{1}{8}$$

$$\frac{1}{2}$$

$$\frac{3}{5}$$

$$\frac{3}{7}$$

$$\frac{3}{9}$$

GLOSSARY

denominator (di-NOM-uh-nay-tor): the bottom number of a fraction that shows the number of equal parts of the whole

equivalent (i-KWIV-uh-luhnt): equal to

fraction (FRAK-shuhn): part of a whole

fraction bar (FRAK-shuhn BAR): the line in a fraction that separates the numerator and the denominator

half (HAF): dividing a number into two equal parts

improper fraction (im-PROP-ur FRAK-shuhn): when a numerator of a fraction is larger than the denominator

mixed number (MIKST NUHM-bur): a number containing a fraction and whole number

numerator (NOO-mu-ray-tur): the top number of a fraction that shows how many parts of the whole are taken

proper fraction (PROP-ur FRAK-shuhn): a fraction whose numerator is smaller than the denominator

whole number (HOLE NUHM-bur): counting numbers beginning with zero

INDEX

denominator(s) 7, 8, 12, 13, 14, 18, 22, 24, 26, 28

equivalent 20, 21

fraction 4-16, 18-29

fraction bar 6, 7

half 8, 14, 15

improper fraction 18, 19

mixed number 16, 17

numerator 6, 8, 12-14, 18, 22, 24, 26, 28

proper fraction 10, 11

whole number 12, 16, 18

WEBSITES TO VISIT

www.bgfl.org/bgfl/custom/resources_ftp/client_ftp/ks2/maths/fractions/
   index.htm
www.bbc.co.uk/skillswise/game/ma17frac-game-dolphin-racing-fractions
www.kidsolr.com/math/fractions.html

ABOUT THE AUTHOR

Lisa Arias is a math teacher who lives in Tampa, Florida with her husband and two children. Her out-of-the-box thinking and teaching style guided her toward becoming an author. She enjoys playing board games and spending time with family and friends.

Meet The Author!
www.meetREMauthors.com

© 2015 Rourke Educational Media

www.rourkeeducationalmedia.com

PHOTO CREDITS: Cover: © soberve; Page 4: © kyoshino; Page 5: ratselmeister

Edited by: Jill Sherman

Cover and Interior design by: Tara Raymo

Library of Congress PCN Data

Fraction Action: Fractions Are Numbers Too / Lisa Arias
(Got Math!)
ISBN 978-1-62717-709-2 (hard cover)
ISBN 978-1-62717-831-0 (soft cover)
ISBN 978-1-62717-944-7 (e-Book)
Library of Congress Control Number: 2014935586

Printed in the United States of America, North Mankato, Minnesota

Also Available as: